I0796248

To My Grandson
with Love

ISBN: 978-1-68088-472-2

and Blue Mountain Press are registered in U.S. Patent and Trademark Office.
Certain trademarks are used under license.

Printed in China.
First Printing: 2024

This book is printed on recycled paper.

This book is printed on paper that has been specially produced to be acid free (neutral pH) and contains no groundwood or unbleached pulp. It conforms with the requirements of the American National Standards Institute, Inc., so as to ensure that this book will last and be enjoyed by future generations.

Blue Mountain Arts, Inc.
P.O. Box 4549, Boulder, Colorado 80306

Susan Polis Schutz

To My Grandson with Love

Blue Mountain Press™
Boulder, Colorado

To My Grandson with Love

I looked at you today
and saw the same sensitive eyes
that looked at me with love
when you were a baby

I looked at you today
and saw the same angelic mouth
that made me cry when you
first smiled at me
when you were a baby
It was not long ago
that I held you in my arms
long after you fell asleep
and I just kept rocking you
Every day is exciting
as I continue to watch you grow
I want you to always know that
in good and bad times
and no matter what you do
or how you think
or what you say
you can depend on
my support, guidance
friendship and love
every minute of every day
I love being your grandparent

I am so happy with the direction
that your life is taking you
You are unique and special
and I know that
your talents will give you
many paths to choose from
in the future
Always keep your many interests —
they will allow your mind
to remain energized
Always keep your positive outlook —
it will give you the strength to
accomplish great things
Always keep your determination —
it will give you the ability
to succeed in meeting your goals
Always keep your excitement
about whatever you do —
it will help you to have fun
Always keep your sense of humor —
it will allow you to
make mistakes and learn from them

Always keep your confidence —
it will allow you to take risks
and not be afraid of failure
Always keep your sensitivity —
it will help you to understand
and do something about
injustices in the world
Always remember that
I am more proud of you
than ever before

I'm Glad to Be Your Grandparent

There is a very special bond
between a grandparent
and grandchild
Both know that
neither is directly responsible for
the behavior of the other
yet the familial tie
is so strong

This results in a
relaxed relationship based on
love and giving into each other completely
Grandparents play games
with their grandchildren
that parents would never play
Grandparents take their grandchildren
to places that parents
would not think of
Grandparents give their grandchildren
an understanding of heritage
that parents cannot give
Grandparents and grandchildren
frolic in happiness in each other's presence
I am so glad to have
this wonderful, unique and
beautiful relationship
with you
my grandchild

I remember
rock, rock, rocking
all my love
into the beautiful miracle
that was you as a baby
hugging you so close
hoping my arms would
protect you from all
struggles
Rock, rock, rocking
as I gazed at this new life
that was you
kissing your little head
hoping that you would always be
as peaceful as you were then
I remember the feel
of your little breaths
against my heart when I held you as a baby
We would inhale together
in unison
Then we would exhale together
in song

I would hold you tightly
so you could feel the security of my arms
I would sing softly to you
so you would know the gentleness
    of my emotions
When your eyes opened
you would look at me for reassurance
Our bonding was boundless
I would kiss your soft cheek
as you peacefully fell asleep
absorbing the enormous love
surrounding you

A grandson is
a kite flying through the trees
a tadpole turning into a frog
a dandelion in the wind
a mischievous smile
laughing eyes
a scrape on the knees
a wonder
an excitement, a burst of energy
an animation
a spirited breeze

A grandson is love
and everything beautiful

What I Love About You

I love your bright face
when we talk seriously about the world
I love your smile
when you laugh at the inconsistencies
    in the world
I love your eyes
when you are showing emotion
I love your mind
when you are discovering new ideas
and creating dreams to follow
I enjoy you so much and
I look forward to any time
we can spend together
Not only are you
    my adored grandson
but you are also my friend

I Love You Dearly

When I think about you
I often wonder what
you will be doing
when you are older
I worry about the harshness of the world
affecting your sensitive ways
You are so kind
so generous
so good
so honest
I hope that you will always be
surrounded by all the
beautiful things in the world

As I watch
with extreme pride and happiness
every step that you take
toward manhood
I want you to know
that I will always
love you dearly

I Am Here for You in Every Way

Sometimes we do not feel
like we want to feel
Sometimes we do not achieve
what we want to achieve
Sometimes things happen
that do not make sense
Sometimes life leads us in directions
that are beyond our control
It is at these times most of all
that we need someone
who will quietly understand us
and be there to support us

I want you to know
that I am here for you
in every way
and remember that though
difficulties may arise
tomorrow is a new day

I will support you
in all that you
do
I will help you
in all that you
need
I will share with you
in all that you
experience
I will encourage you
in all that you
try
I will understand you
in all that is in your
heart
I will love you
in all that you
are

Grandson, Just Do Your Best and Know That Is Enough

Sometimes you
think that you
need to be perfect
that you cannot
make mistakes
At these times
you put so much
pressure on yourself
Try to realize
that you are
a human being
like everyone else —
capable of
reaching great potential
but not capable of
being perfect
Just do your best
and realize that
this is enough

It is so important
to let your feelings
be known
Talk to someone
Write your feelings down
Create something
based on your feelings
but do not keep them inside
Never be afraid to
be honest with people
And certainly never
be afraid to
be honest with yourself

You are such an
interesting, sensitive
intelligent person
who has so much to share

I want you to know
that wherever you go
or whatever you do
or whatever you think
you can always depend
on me
for complete and absolute
understanding
support
and love
forever

In This Constantly Changing World...

A family can give you
the freedom and backing
to go out in the world
and become a success
at whatever you want to do

A family is a structure built on love
from which you will
forever have support

A family is a relationship
that will grow through
good and bad times

A family is a commitment
to help each other and
to be as happy as possible in life

A family is a security that one
might not otherwise have
in the vast world

A family is thousands of
shared experiences

A family is inspirational

A family can give you the needed
confidence and happiness
to achieve great things
in the world

Ever since you were born
you have been a bundle of
perpetual motion
Your energy is endless
Your mind is unbounded
You want to touch, smell, feel
and do everything
You want to live life to the fullest

But don't forget
you are extraordinarily creative
and it is hard for creativity to flourish
unless there is a certain amount
of quietness and peace
So you will, at times, need to quell
your vigor
stop your movements
and let the perpetual motion of your mind
leap to new bounds
as you bask in the stillness of your
spirit and soul

Take Time To...

Lean against a tree
and dream your world of dreams
Work hard at what you like to do
and try to overcome all obstacles

Laugh at your mistakes
and praise yourself for learning from them
Pick some flowers
and appreciate the beauty of nature
Be honest with people
and enjoy the good in them
Don't be afraid to show your emotions
Laughing and crying make you feel better
Love your friends and family with your
entire being
They are the most important part of your life
Feel the calmness on a quiet sunny day
and plan what you want to accomplish in life
Find a rainbow
and live your
world of dreams

Live in the Present and Make the Most of Every Day

Appreciate every moment
Dance
Sing
Play
Create
Love
Give
Help
Don't worry
Live in the present
Do not be a reflection of the rain
Be a reflection of the sun

If you make your own goals
if you adhere to your own values
if you choose your own kind of fun
you are living a life made by you
If other people are telling you what to do
or if you are copying other people's ways
or if you are acting out a certain lifestyle
    to impress people
you are living for other people rather than
    for yourself

People should not control you —
you must control your own life

Do What's Right for You

You cannot listen
to what others
want you to do
You must listen
to yourself
Society
family
friends
and loved ones
do not know what
you must do
Only you know
and only you
can do what is
right for you

Do what you want to do
Be what you want to be
Look the way you want to look
Act the way you want to act

Think the way you want to think
Speak the way you want to speak
Follow the goals you want to follow

Live according to the truths within yourself

Find Happiness in Everything You Do

Find happiness in nature
in the beauty of a mountain
in the serenity of the sea
Find happiness in friendship
in the fun of doing things together
in the sharing and understanding
Find happiness in your family
in the stability of knowing
    that someone cares
in the strength of love and honesty
Find happiness in yourself
in your mind and body
in your values and achievements
Find happiness in everything
you do

My Dear Grandson, May You Always Know Love

Love is the strongest feeling known
an all-encompassing passion
an extreme strength
an overwhelming excitement

Love is trying not to hurt the other person
trying not to change the other person
trying not to dominate the other person
trying not to deceive the other person

Love is understanding each other
listening to each other
supporting each other
having fun with each other

Love is not an excuse to stop growing
not an excuse to stop making yourself better
not an excuse to lessen one's goals
not an excuse to take the other person for granted

Love is being completely honest with each other
finding dreams to share
working toward common goals
sharing responsibilities equally

Everyone in the world wants to love
Love is not a feeling to be taken lightly
Love is a feeling to be cherished
nurtured and cared for
Love is
the reason for life

I Wish You Success in All You Do

What an incredible young person
you are growing up to be
I was proud of you when you were born
I was proud of you when you were
a young child

Now as you continue
to grow in your own
unique, wonderful way
I am more proud of you
than ever before
Whatever happens in the future
I will always be wishing
for your happiness
and success
and at all times
I want you to know
that you have
my unconditional support
and love

Grandson, I Love You

To see you happy —
laughing and joking
smiling and content
striving toward goals of your own
accomplishing what you set out to do
having fun
capable of loving and being loved
is what I always wished for you

Today I thought about your
    precious face
and felt your excitement for life
and your genuine happiness
and I burst with pride
as I realized that my dreams
    for you have come true

What an extraordinary person
you have become
and as you continue to grow
please remember always
how very much
I love you

About the Author

Susan Polis Schutz is an accomplished writer, poet, documentary filmmaker, and advocate for women's issues, the elderly, and dispelling the stigma of mental illness. She is a graduate of Rider University where she majored in English and biology and was later awarded an honorary doctor of laws degree. Together with her husband, Stephen Schutz, she cofounded Blue Mountain Arts, a popular publisher known for its distinctive greeting cards, gifts, and poetry books.

Susan is the author of many best-selling books of poetry illustrated by Stephen, including *To My Daughter with Love on the Important Things in Life*, which has sold over 1.8 million copies. Its companion volume, *To My Son with Love*, has also enjoyed a wide audience. Susan's poems and Stephen's artwork have been published on over 435 million greeting cards worldwide.

Susan's latest undertaking is creating documentary films that make a difference in people's lives with her production company, IronZeal Films. Her films have been shown on PBS stations throughout the country and include *The Misunderstood Epidemic: Depression*, which seeks to bring greater attention to this debilitating illness, and *Over 90 and Loving It*, which features people in their 90s and 100s who are living extraordinary and passionate lives. Her newest film, *Love wins over hate*, explores the lives of six former white supremacists and ultraconservatives. Each tells of their transformation from being filled with hate, anger, and rage to acceptance and appreciation of diversity.